Exemplar High Grade GCSE Answers for 'An Inspector Calls' – The Characters

By Laurie Ashwell

Essays linking an analysis of characters from
J.B. Priestley's play to its context.

Contents

Preface	Page 4
[1] Arthur Birling	Page 8
[2] Sybil Birling	Page 15
[3] Sheila Birling	Page 22
[4] Eric Birling	Page 29
[5] Gerald Croft	Page 37
[6] The Inspector	Page 46
[7] Eva Smith	Page 54

3

Laurie Ashwell

Preface

How can you get a grade 9 in English literature GCSE? There is no magic formula. But you need to be someone who reads a lot and understands what you read. You also need to be good at writing – be able to communicate your thoughts eloquently and succinctly with an appropriately academic tone and a range of vocabulary at your disposal. There is, of course, a correlation between reading proficiency and writing proficiency.

But, you also need to be a good thinker – someone whose reflections on a text are perceptive and insightful, and someone who is able to think about the question they are being asked in the exam and know how they ought to answer it.

If you do not already fulfil the above criteria, only reading this book is unlikely to help you write an answer worth a grade 9 for the *An Inspector Calls* question in your English Literature GCSE.

Laurie Ashwell

However, if you are currently hitting high grades and are looking for ways to nudge your way up to a grade 9, this book may provide you with some ideas for how to achieve that: the ideas, the phrases and vocabulary used, the way aspects of the text are linked to its context, and the way evidence and quotations is discussed may help you to develop and improve your own responses. Students often want to see model answers, and it is hoped that the model answers presented in this book will be useful to high performing students.

A word of warning: with each essay provided in this book clocking a word count of over 1000 words it is unlikely that you would be able to recreate the applicable essay, word for word, in the exam. And of course, the essay may not directly address the question you are given in the exam. It would be foolish, therefore, to try and memorise and regurgitate these essays in the exam. But, as stated above, these essays may elevate your own understanding of the characters and develop your own answers on them.

Laurie Ashwell

The exam board which I particularly had in mind while writing these essays was Edexcel, and this particular exam board places a great importance in the mark scheme on the degree to which students are able to link their knowledge of the text to its context. The essays, therefore, routinely investigate the text's presentation of each character and then, subsequently, discuss how that aspect of the character relates to the text's context. However, it is important that students are clear about which exam board they are using and what the requirements are of that exam board – mark schemes do differ.

You will notice when reading each essay that each essay is separated out into three sections with a single line space signifying the division between these sections. Each section discusses a different aspect of the character in question, with exploration of supporting evidence, including quotation, and then makes a contextual link.

Happy reading – I hope you find the essays interesting and useful. And, of course, good luck with that exam!

Laurie Ashwell

[1] **Arthur Birling**

Explore the importance of Mr Birling in *An Inspector Calls*.

You must refer to the context of the play in your answer.

Mr Birling is presented as having poor relationships with his family. This is shown when Eric and Mr Birling argue during the third act. Eric becomes very confrontational when his father asks him why he did not come to him for help when he was in trouble and needed money for Eva Smith. Eric berates at his father, telling him he is 'not the kind of father a chap could go to when he's in trouble, that's why!' Eric's exclamatory outburst shows that Mr Birling has failed to be a supportive father and also highlights one of the themes of the play – the

8

Laurie Ashwell

division between the younger and older generations. Although this narrative event occurs near the end of the Inspector's interrogation, the division between Mr Birling and his children is hinted at more subtly early in act 1. For example, Birling says to Eric, 'Just you keep out of this' and tells Sheila that the conversation has 'nothing to do with you'. These kinds of comments suggest to the audience that Mr Birling is dismissive of his children. As the narrative continues, the cracks in the relationship between Mr Birling and his children widen.

This reflects how, in the early 20th century, those in powerful positions (like Mr Birling) often showed little value for those they ought to be responsible (like their children). Perhaps, symbolically, the writer is making a comment about how the conservative government of the early 1940s had a poor relationship with those it should work to support and protect, especially the working class. Additionally, perhaps the writer presents Mr Birling as having a poor relationship with his children in order to highlight the rift between the older and younger generations in society. It could be argued that Priestley believes that the older generations have caused this rift and are largely unaware of how this leads to a dysfunctional society. Mr Birling is, therefore, important because he is used to highlight how oblivious the older generations are of the division they have created between themselves and the younger generations.

Another reason why Mr Birling is important to the play is because he reveals how capitalists perceive and mistreat the working class. This is shown while he is interrogated by the Inspector and explains his reaction to Eva Smith leading a failed strike for an increase in wages. For example, he says he told her to 'clear out' and made a point of 'com[ing] down sharply' on her. The adverb 'sharply' communicates Mr Birling's intolerant attitude towards members of the working class who seek to address the exploitation from which they suffer. In Mr Birling's mind, the working class, if allowed to do so, would 'soon be asking for the earth'. The hyperbole here exaggerates the aims of the working class who simply requested a moderate increase in salary to '25 shillings a week'. Arguably, this hyperbole infers Mr Birling's fear of the working class empowering themselves through industrial action and recalibrating the imbalance of power between the classes. Furthermore, he clearly understands how destitute his workers are since he acknowledges that those on strike were likely to 'be all broke' after the holidays. With this understanding, his failure to meet their demands appears to the audience to be all the more heartless, ruthless, and driven by a self-serving desire for financial superiority and security.

These attitudes towards those he employs reflects what Priestley believes to be the typical attitudes of business owners and employers. Indeed, the Labour Party victory in the 1945 general election (the year the play was written) is often attributed to the working class's widespread dissatisfaction with their employers and the Labour Party pledging to address workers' rights and support trade unions. As is highlighted through the character of Mr

Birling, employers rarely felt sympathy for their employees despite being responsible for imposing a life of poverty upon them through meagre wages and poor job security. Perhaps Priestley used the character of Mr Birling to raise awareness amongst his audiences of the heartless and apathetic manner in which businesses exploited their workers under the guise of 'a duty to keep labour costs down'.

Finally, Mr Birling is important to the play because of the way he is presented as ignorant and foolish. This is shown early on in the play when speaking to the younger characters, airing his views on a range of topics. With the play set over 30 years before it was written, audiences may have felt amused by Mr Birling's repeated failure to accurately forecast world events. For example, he claims 'there isn't a chance of war', and that there would be a time of 'steadily increasing prosperity', and that by 1940, the world would have 'forgotten all these Capital versus Labour agitations'. Being acutely aware of the two World Wars, the Great Depression and the rise of socialism, an audience in 1945 would have viewed Mr Birling with derision, and with each mistake he makes, his pomposity appears all the more ridiculous. Priestley, therefore, uses dramatic irony to establish Mr Birling as a pompous fool who lacks foresight. For audiences, Mr Birling is presented as a satirical figure of folly; his persistently erroneous judgement is comical, and aids the writer in ridiculing those who would aspire to positions of social power.

Mr Birling's unreliability in foreseeing any of the major calamities of the early twentieth century is meant, by Priestley, to reflect a general lack of foresight in the ruling classes during the early twentieth century. Perhaps Priestley is not merely suggesting that the UK blundered into these disasters, but communicating a belief that many of the major disasters of the early twentieth century (and, of course, disasters that took place at an individual level) could have been averted had the ruling classes assessed the direction in which they were steering society more shrewdly. The

Laurie Ashwell

Inspector intends the other characters to consider the consequences of their actions – to recognise that one person's actions can create 'a chain of events' which can, ultimately, lead to tragedy. Mr Birling's foolishness highlights Priestley's concern that the ruling classes will never act responsibly if they are wont to dismiss the possibility of tragedy as an outcome.

[2] <u>Sybil Birling</u>

Explore the importance of Mrs Birling in *An Inspector Calls*.

You must refer to the context of the play in your answer.

Mrs Birling is presented as a character who is prejudiced against members of the lower class. This is shown most clearly during her interrogation during act 2. For example, she communicates a predisposition to believing that members of the lower class are inherently less civilised than members of the middle and upper classes: she states that Eva Smith was claiming 'elaborate fine feelings and scruples that were simply absurd in a girl in her position'. Here, Mrs Birling expounds a belief that a person's social class directly correlates with their ability to live by a set of moral principles. Mrs Birling refused to believe that Eva Smith, being 'a girl of that sort', would refuse stolen money. Because Eva Smith's persona did not dovetail with Mrs Birling's prejudiced beliefs, Mrs Birling refused her charity's assistance, sealing Eva Smith's tragic fate. Interestingly, Mrs Birling uses euphemism to refer to the lower class in the above quotations – 'a girl in her position' and 'a girl of that sort'. This can be read as a sign of her abhorrence for the lower echelons of society, with the euphemism being a result of her loathing to explicitly refer to lower classes.

A parallel can be drawn between Mrs Birling's failure, as the head of a charity, to support a vulnerable lady and worthy cause, with the way Priestley perceives prime ministers of successive Conservative governments to have failed in their duty to protect and support the most vulnerable members of society. Arguably, Mrs Birling is important to the play because Priestley uses her to highlight the hypocrisy of the ruling elite: the conservative leaders of the early 20th century viewed the harsh conditions and widespread poverty in which the lower classes worked and lived as unfortunate, yet were reluctant to intervene. For Priestley, and other socialists, the Conservatives were ducking their responsibility, and Priestley's characterisation of Mrs Birling as prejudiced may explain what he believed laid at the root of this governmental lethargy.

Mrs Birling is presented as a character whose perceptions of reality are inaccurate and naïve. One way in which this is communicated is through how revelations regarding her son leave her shocked. For example, in act 2, the stage directions describe Mrs Birling to be 'staggered' to learn from Gerald that Eric drinks 'pretty hard'. But later, when Mrs Birling finally realises that Eric was the father of Eva's unborn child, Mrs Birling cries out 'I don't believe it. I *won't* believe it.' The negative auxiliary verb 'won't' highlights Mrs Birling's aversion to the truth; the reality of Eric's drunken sexual involvement with a woman from the lower class, and, in addition to this, the suggestion that he stole money is too unpalatable for Mrs Birling to contemplate, thus leaving her to declare her denial of the ugly truth. But, importantly, her surprise is not limited to revelations regarding the questionable behaviour of her immediate family and Gerald: when Gerald states that Aldermand Meggarty is 'one of the worst sots and rogues in Brumley' Mrs Birling is again 'staggered', as stated by the stage directions. Priestley, therefore, presents Mrs Birling as a character who is shocked to learn that members of the middle and upper classes with whom she associates have behaved dishonourably and unethically. Particularly in regards to her son, the reality of his actions becomes a bitter pill that she never quite swallows.

While Mrs Birling is, perhaps, owing to her defiance, prejudice and cruelty, the character who has the least redeeming features, audiences may still feel an element of sympathy for her in respect to her inaccurate and naïve perceptions of reality. She is shocked by the behaviour of others because she holds the middle and upper classes in such high regard. Arguably, her naivety is forgivable as the dishonourable or immoral behaviour that surprises her has been deliberately concealed. Interestingly, it is privileged men rather than privileged women whose reprehensible actions are conducted covertly – Gerald, Eric and (by implication) Aldermand Meggarty all sought to hide their mistreatment of women; Mrs Birling and Sheila conducted their mistreatment of Eva Smith quite openly. Regardless of the gender politics Priestley raises in this way, Mrs Birling's shock when faced with the reality of middle and upper class debauchery relays a message about the way a sizeable proportion of the privileged sections of male society conducts itself and how a notable proportion of privileged female society remains blissfully ignorant. For Priestley, in order for the middle and upper classes to embrace the social changes he desires, those classes must develop a higher level of self-awareness, recognising its own degeneracy in order to address it.

Mrs Birling is presented as the character that is resistant to change. This is shown during her interrogation as well as

Laurie Ashwell

after Gerald suggests the Inspector was a hoax. For example, while being questioned, she repeatedly declares her innocence with statements such as 'I did nothing I'm ashamed of', 'I was perfectly justified' and 'I accept no blame for it at all'. The frequency of declarative statements such as these communicates Mrs Birling's staunch intention not to concede any success for the Inspector in evoking her sense of guilt. Mrs Birling continues to affirm her innocence after the Inspector has left with more declarative statements such as 'I had done no more than my duty'. By misrepresenting her cruelty as her 'duty', Mrs Birling appears to the audience as brutally heartless and conceited. In her final line in the play, she patronises Eric and Sheila by saying that 'in the morning they'll be as amused as we are'. With this final condescending remark, Mrs Birling's resistance to change appears to the audience to be all the more foolish.

Mrs Birling's resistance to change reflects what Priestley believed to be an attitude that existed in a section of the middle and upper classes during the early twentieth century. He believed that many of these more privileged people refused to recognise that the way they treated the more vulnerable sections of society was morally repugnant. Moreover, Mrs Birling's character indicates that Priestley consider such people to be averse to change because, in contrast to a socialist ideology, they do not believe that they – the upper classes – hold any responsibility to support or protect those who are from more disadvantaged backgrounds. But Priestley's criticism of such people extends beyond the margins of political discourse – it is not simply that these people are *anti-socialist* in their politics, but, as discussed above, that they are prejudiced, cruel and cold-hearted in their conduct towards those who, like Eva Smith, find themselves in 'alone, friendless, almost penniless, [and] desperate'. While Priestley emphasises the hope he has for a progressive, socialist and compassionate society through the characters of Eric and Sheila, Mrs Birling in particular, along with her husband and Gerald, symbolise a dark shadow that is cast over the playwright's hope for change.

[3] <u>Sheila Birling</u>

Explore the importance of Sheila in *An Inspector Calls.*

You must refer to the context of the play in your answer.

After recognizing the flaws in her attitude towards the lower classes, Sheila develops a moral and mature response to the narrative events that follow. For example, after the revelation that Gerald was unfaithful to her, Sheila's reaction is decisive and measured. The stage directions describe how Sheila 'hands' back the ring, thus breaking off the engagement. The verb 'hands' shows how Sheila acts without anger and with control. Her following speech also presents her as a reflective and considerate character as she both acknowledges, and almost praises Gerald for being 'honest', while condemning Gerald for 'lying' to her. Her response is therefore considered and civil, thus presenting her as mature and moral.

This mode of behaviour stands in direct contrast with the more hysterical and pompous behaviour of her parents. Mr Birling, for example, appears to react to revelations regarding other characters' interactions with Eva Smith impulsively. When Mrs Birling explains why she was 'prejudiced' against Eva Smith, Mr Birling replies by saying 'And I should think so! Damned impudence!' Priestley's use of exclamation marks in exclamatory sentences presents Mr Birling as overwrought and lacking self-control, which contrasts with Sheila's calm and controlled language. Similarly, Mrs Birling's reaction to finding out her son, Eric, was responsible for Eva Smith's pregnancy is one of distress and denial – 'I don't believe it. I won't believe it.' Again, in contrast to Sheila, Mrs Birling lacks an even-tempered response.

Laurie Ashwell

This juxtaposition in the style of characters' language could have been engineered by Priestley as part of his attempt to persuade audiences to favour characters such as Sheila. Her development, being representative of a political shift towards socialism is set in contrast to characters such as Mr and Mrs Birling who symbolise a more stubborn and fixed mindset, firmly supportive of conservative and capitalist values. Sheila is presented as sensible and intelligent. Through portraying Sheila in this positive way, through her style of language, Priestley attempts to sway the audience's bias towards the social and political values she comes to represent, and away from those of Mr and Mrs Birling.

Although Priestley therefore presents Sheila as even-tempered and thoughtful, importantly, she is still portrayed to have emotional responses to the discoveries of the other characters' misdemeanours: when Mrs Birling admits to refusing to provide support to Eva Smith, Sheila's assertion that her mother's actions were 'cruel and vile' communicates a revulsion for the apathy her mother has demonstrated. Significantly, after the Inspector has left and Mr Birling, Mrs Birling and Gerald begin to question the Inspector's credentials and the credibility behind his claims of a suicide, Sheila refuses to revert to a state of apathy, regardless of the truth, because of 'what he made [her] feel' – the emotional response that the Inspector evoked in her was powerful enough to permanently secure her development of a social conscience.

Sheila's emotionally charged behaviour is important to the play, particularly when considered alongside the Inspector's professional, and therefore reserved, approach to his investigation. The Inspector remains calm and avoids hostility while he systematically exposes the flaws in each character's views and behaviour: when criticizing Mr Birling, for example, the Inspector's language avoids directly accusing Mr Birling of the fault of which he speaks – 'Public men, Mr Birling, have responsibilities as well as privileges'. Sheila is therefore an important character because she adds an emotional dimension to the play's socialist voice, complementing the professional and reserved tone of the Inspector; if the Inspector is at the play's political centre, Sheila is at the play's emotional centre.

Again, the portrayal of Sheila as an emotional character can be seen as part of Priestley's attempts to persuade the audience to adopt socialist values. Certainly, the Inspector sympathizes with Eva Smith and his condemnation of the other characters' behaviour is made clear in act 3 when his language becomes didactic – 'We don't live alone… We are responsible for each other.' But his authority is balanced by Sheila's emotion and sentimentality which humanizes the play's socialist voice. Priestley intended audiences to identify with Sheila's humanity, warming to her character and, correspondingly, warming to her new socialist beliefs. A final reason why Sheila is important to the play is because she acts as a representation of women that are strong-minded and growing in independence and moral fortitude. The two main female characters – Sheila and Mrs Birling – are, indeed, characters who exhibit strength in their own right. However, the opposition between Sheila and her mother provides audiences with opposing representations of women – Sheila being a woman who comes to embody feminist values and Mrs Birling who appears anti-feminist.

Quite early on in the play, Sheila shows an innate duty to support the rights of other women. Even before she realizes how she contributed to the downfall of Eva Smith, in response to her father's treatment of Eva Smith, Sheila states that 'these girls aren't cheap labour – they're people'. While Mrs Birling is characterized as a woman who is not dependent upon her husband, despite tradition, she is not presented as the kind of woman others should aspire to become. Her flaw is her apathy, and her refusal to support Eva Smith and offer her charitable assistance is indicative of a woman who has no compassion for women in a precariously vulnerable position.

Sheila recognizes that her mother 'hardened [Eva Smith's] heart and gave her the final push that finished her'. Sheila, therefore, realizes that women who enjoy positions of authority have a duty to protect and assist more vulnerable women, thus aligning herself with the feminist movement of the early 20th century. With women gaining increasing levels of equality with men, society was beginning to recognize that women were capable of assuming positions of responsibility in society, such as members of parliament. Priestley presents a contrast and conflict between the compassionate ideals of Sheila and the apathetic and prejudiced views of her mother. He reminds the audience that without compassion, women's aspirations for a shared balance of power in society between the sexes are a departure from feminist ideals.

[4] **Eric Birling**

Explore the importance of Eric in *An Inspector Calls*.

You must refer to the context of the play in your answer.

Eric is important to the play because his treatment of Eva Smith reveals how vulnerable women were liable to fall victim to abusive men. This is shown during Eric's interrogation when his confession of misconduct implies that he raped Eva Smith. He tells the Inspector that he 'insisted' on accompanying her to her lodgings and, when she asked him not to enter he 'was in that state when a chap easily turns nasty – and [he] threatened to make a row'. The verbs 'insisted' and 'threatened' suggest that Eric behaved forcefully towards Eva Smith and dismissed her wishes in a selfish pursuit of sexual gratification. While not directly stated, the implication is that Eric forced Eva Smith into sexual intercourse without her consent. Although, arguably, both Eric and Gerald could be described as men that used Eva Smith as a sexual object for their own gratification, Eric is the only character whose mistreatment of Eva Smith can be truly termed as physically abusive, leaving her violated and pregnant.

Eric's act of sexual abuse reflects the harsh reality of inequality between the genders during the early twentieth century; by forcing a woman into sexual intercourse, Eric shows utter disregard for her rights and personal autonomy. In 1912, when the play was set, the suffragette movement was well established. While that movement was focused upon securing equality between the genders in terms of democratic voting, Priestley is undoubtedly highlighting how inequality existed in other forms during this time, with men, despite its illegality, assuming an unwritten right to demand women submit to their sexual advances.

Priestley's presentation of the sexual dominance of the patriarchy and its resulting injustices is intensified by the dynamics of social class between Eva and Eric. With the play having already established a pattern of mistreatment of the lower class by the higher classes, Eric's sexual assault of Eva Smith appears all the more opportunistic and ruthless as not only an act of misogyny, but also another example of the privileged exploiting the vulnerability of the disadvantaged.

Eric is important to the play because his fractious relationships with his family creates tension for the audience. Certainly, the bickering between Eric and Sheila at the play's opening adds amusement for the audience. But, it is the conflict between Eric and both his parents that creates tension in the final act of the play. In part, this is caused by revelations of Eric's tendency to conceal his vices and transgressions: his drinking, sexual assault of Eva Smith, and theft of fifty pounds. When Eric's father berates Eric, calling him a 'damned fool', and questions why Eric didn't approach him for help, Eric retorts by saying that he is 'not the kind of father a chap could go to when he's in trouble'. Here, the dysfunctionality of the Birling family is laid bare by Eric. Eric's belligerence is also aimed at his mother: when learning of her failure to assist Eva Smith he exclaims 'damn you… You don't understand anything. You never did. You never even tried…'. Here, Eric's repetition of the pronoun 'you' creates a confrontational atmosphere, signalling the disintegration of the façade that fronted his relationship with his mother. As with his father, Eric, again, feels unsupported by his mother. As these relationships break down, the drama becomes increasingly contrasted with the celebratory tone of the play's opening and the conflict within the family becomes progressively irreconcilable.

The dysfunctional relationship between Eric and his parents could be seen as symbolic of a conflict and lack of unity that Priestley recognises within the higher classes. As the play progresses, Eric and Sheila become united in their sense of guilt and

32

Laurie Ashwell

newfound sense of personal responsibility, forming an alliance that challenges the apathy of their parents and Gerald in the final act. Eric's confrontational manner and accusations against his parents in act 3 feed into a generational conflict that is unearthed throughout the play. Through Eric's belligerent behaviour, arguably, Priestley is highlighting a disharmony that exists between the younger an older generations of the higher classes, and a growing dissatisfaction of the younger generations in how those who should have nurtured and supported them, neglected and dismissed them. Without doubt, Priestley considers the younger generations as more receptive to socialism than the older generations; as the Inspector comments: 'We often do [make an impression] on the young ones'. But Eric's confrontation of his parents may well symbolise what Priestley believes to be an inevitable clash between the generations; as the younger generations assume the mantle of perpetuating the socialist movement, deep-seated grievances with those who resist and challenge them can no longer be suppressed.

Finally, Eric is important to the play because he is one of the two characters who, by the end of the play, have developed a social conscience. As with Sheila, Eric's development of a social conscience is initiated by the overwhelming sense of guilt he experiences on realising that his mistreatment of Eva Smith moved her closer to suicide. In act 3, Eric persistently laments Eva's death, showing his anguish for the tragic loss of life. For example, using repetition of a morbid motif, he says lines such as 'the girl's dead isn't she?', 'the one I knew is dead' and 'nobody's brought her to life'. It could be argued that, despite Eric's abhorrent mistreatment of Eva Smith, he fundamentally believes in the value of human life. This respect for human life is why, when he realises that his actions pushed her closer to suicide, his guilt overwhelms him, endowing him with a newfound social conscience, but also leaving him traumatised by the reality of her death. For the audience, Eric's constant preoccupation with his grief communicates his humanity – a humanity that is lacking in his parents and Gerald. Through lamenting the tragedy involved in the loss of a human life, Eric continues an idea raised earlier in the play when Sheila asserts that working class people are not just 'cheap labour – they're people'; Eric has learned the hard way that when the humanity of the vulnerable people of society is forgotten or disregarded, and their weakness is exploited, the extent of the consequential suffering of such people can be extreme, and even fatal.

Eric's distress over Eva's death is, therefore, integral to the growth of his socialist ideology. It could be argued that Priestley believes that, in order for the higher classes to recalibrate their attitudes, and create and build a society that supports and protects its most vulnerable citizens, they must first feel pained by how they have instead exploited and harmed them. For Priestley, the way that women were at risk of being abused and mistreated by men was abhorrent, and this abhorrence must be recognised by its perpetrators. Perhaps Priestley's message for the audience is that the suffering that the more powerful echelons of society impose upon the more vulnerable ranks, should, when exposed, cause embarrassment, shame and distress. If the higher classes lack the humanity that Eric displays when confronted with the ugly consequences of their indifference and apathy – if their moral compass is not guided by the basic respect for human life that Eric holds – they will be unable to embrace the central tenets of socialism.

[5] **Gerald Croft**

Explore the importance of Gerald in *An Inspector Calls*.

You must refer to the context of the play in your answer.

Gerald is an important character because he represents the existence of deceit and duplicity within the upper class. His deceitful nature is hinted at from early in act 1 when Sheila complains of how Gerald 'never came near [her]' during the previous summer. However, immediately prior to his confession, the extent of Gerald's duplicity is laid bare before the audience when he attempts to persuade Sheila – the woman to whom he has been unfaithful – to lie for him in order to 'keep it from' the Inspector. Here, with his deception of Sheila made clear, and in declaring his intention to coordinate further deception, Gerald's duplicitous nature could easily appear habitual to the audience. Interestingly, Gerald never clearly states why he chose to have an affair in secret with Daisy Renton rather than end his relationship with Sheila and enjoy his relationship with Daisy more publicly. However, in light of the systemic discrimination of the lower classes by the higher classes that the play highlights elsewhere, and Mrs Birling's assertion that the affair was 'disgusting', we could assume that Gerald's mendacity stems from a belief that a relationship traversing the boundary of the class division would have been met by criticism and ridicule by his social peers. Gerald's deceit is therefore a consequence of his conceited attempts to maintain a respectable reputation.

It can be argued that Priestley uses the character of Gerald, and his mendacious tendencies, to make a statement about the higher classes' sense of superiority and respectability. Perhaps, through characters such as Gerald and Eric, who also conceals digressions such as theft, alcohol abuse and rape, Priestley intends to suggest to the audience that the behaviour of the higher classes may not be as respectable and civilised as the public image they aim to project; Priestley wishes the audience to recognise that the outward appearance of someone like a successful businessman from a rich and reputable family may not be a truthful representation of their actual identity, of which the more repugnant aspects have been kept hidden. Therefore, Priestley's message for the audience may be that a belief that equates the upper classes with moral fortitude and trustworthiness would be naïvely overlooking their capacity to lie, cheat and deceive.

However, Priestley portrays Gerald as a complex character to whom, at moments, the audience is likely to warm towards. During his interrogation, Gerald is portrayed as compassionate and affectionate; when compelled to reveal the truth about his affair, he describes what his feelings were for Daisy Renton, exposing a tender and sensitive dynamic to his personality. For example, he insists he provided Daisy with accommodation because he 'was sorry for her, and didn't like the idea of her going back to the Palace bar'. Here, Gerald appears genuinely concerned for Daisy's welfare and, with the Palace bar being 'a favourite haunt of women of the town', the suggestion is that Gerald was protecting Daisy from being forced into a life of prostitution. A further example of Gerald's integrity is when he directly refutes Mrs Birling's condemnation of the relationship, declaring that the affair 'wasn't disgusting'. Arguably, when Gerald defends the affair, refusing to allow Mrs Birling to brand it immoral and unwholesome, he is asserting that the affair was founded upon genuine and mutual affection, rather than lust and exploitation. Furthermore, if we view Mrs Birling's revulsion towards the relationship to stem from an aversion towards sexual unions that traverse the boundary of the class division, the strength of conviction in Gerald's rebuttal implies Gerald views the lower classes with a sense of equity; he values their humanity in a way

Laurie Ashwell

that Mrs Birling does not. With this suggestion that, when it comes to relationships, he is loath to discriminate, and in the moments when Gerald displays his affections and compassion for Daisy, audiences are likely to find Gerald an endearing character.

Gerald's compassion and integrity is important to the narrative because, through Gerald, Priestley is making a statement about the existence of kindness and moral fortitude that he believes is present within a proportion of the higher classes, but also, as with Gerald, this kindness and moral fortitude is often not exhibited publically. Perhaps Priestley believed that if those in the upper classes were more open and publicly vocal about their sympathies for the lower classes' struggle for survival, and, indeed, their compulsion to save and support them, the suffering of the lower classes could be more efficiently resolved. Significantly, although Gerald withdrew the support he provided for Daisy, which ultimately left her in more desperate circumstances, he is the only character who approached her with kindness and compassion. This is important as it implies that Priestley does not wish to tar everyone from the middle and upper classes with the same brush by oversimplifying the stance of the more privileged sections of society; while the discrimination and exploitation of the lower classes was endemic in the early 20th century, Priestley is careful not to stereotype the middle and upper classes as apathetic.

Although Gerald, therefore, displays differing qualities which are both appealing and unappealing for audiences, ultimately, Gerald is the character who most disappoints audiences. This is a result of the contrasting presentation of his character directly before he leaves the stage to 'walk about' and after he returns. When Gerald requests permission from the Inspector 'to be alone for a while' he appears to have been humbled by the interrogation. This is not only shown through the act of seeking permission from the Inspector, which tacitly acknowledges the Inspector's authority over him, but also by the language he uses when responding to Sheila: 'But I'm coming back – if I may'. Here, the additional clause at the end of this sentence shifts the declarative sentence into a conditional sentence that politely seeks Sheila's authorisation, thus inferring a newfound meekness in his character. In this submissive and melancholic state, audiences may even pity Gerald as he exits the stage.

However, on his return in act 3, such endearing qualities are strikingly absent from Gerald's character as he expounds theories that, he believes, relieves each of them from any sense of responsibility for their respective indiscretions: it is Gerald who claims the Inspector was not actually a real police inspector, and who questions whether the girl they all wronged was the same girl, and who suggests a suicide may not have actually occurred. His loss of humility, shame and sorrow is further amplified by his flippant attitude: when Sheila tells Gerald that he doesn't yet know 'the rest of [their] crimes and idiocies', Gerald replies 'that's all right, I don't want to', thus appearing dismissive and uninterested. Indeed, after implying that he had genuine affection for Daisy in act 2, his unaffectionate language in act 3 diminishes the high-regard he held for Daisy when he states 'I did keep a girl last summer'. Here, the verb 'keep' reduces Daisy to a possession or pet, dehumanising the woman who previously humanised Gerald in act 2. Guided by his conceit, Gerald seeks to expunge himself of responsibility for his transgressions, creating a stark shift in his attitude, actions and language – a shift that greatly disappoints the audience.

Gerald's reversal in behaviour reflects what Priestley fears was hindering the socialist movement in the early twentieth century – the self-preservation of the conceited middle and upper classes. Gerald's attempt to nullify his, and the others' moral transgressions reeks of apathy towards those who fall victim to the cruelty of the rich and powerful and a selfish drive to maintain a sense of righteous superiority in society. Priestley uses Gerald to present his fear that the socialist movement, which requires the upper and middle classes to accept that the divide between the rich and the poor, and between men and women, needs addressing, may be stifled by an almost instinctual and habitual resistance to social responsibility. If the majority of those in power found it preferable to protect their supercilious sense of self-worth, rather than entertain ideas regarding personal and social responsibility, threatening their pride and unveiling their flaws, the progress of socialism would be impeded. If anything, Gerald's character suggests that Priestley believes people can easily traverse between capitalist and socialist ideologies, and that not all of the younger generations will be so easily converted as Eric and Sheila.

[6] **The Inspector**

Explore the importance of The Inspector in *An Inspector Calls*.

You must refer to the context of the play in your answer.

The Inspector is an important character because he is critical of the other characters, and by being so, he undermines their carte blanche attitudes. This is shown throughout the play, such as when Mr Birling claims that it is necessary to 'come down sharply on these people' to avoid them 'asking for the earth'. The Inspector's rebuttal extends the metaphor: '...it's better to ask for the earth than to take it'. This implies, albeit subtly, that the Inspector views Mr Birling, and perhaps all business owners alike, as having taken control of society through the power they wield as employers; the idea of Mr Birling '*taking*' the earth suggests that the acquisition of this power was an act of misappropriation.

A further example of the Inspector's critical voice in act one is when he responds to Gerald's assertion that they are 'respectable citizens and not criminals'. He replies 'sometimes there isn't as much difference as you think. Often... I wouldn't know where to draw the line'. Again, without making his criticism of the characters too direct, the Inspector reveals his propensity not to correlate social status with a level of assumed respect. Here, the Inspector shows Gerald that he will not allow the social status of Gerald or the Birlings to prejudice his investigation – no one, no matter the height of their social standing, can act with impunity.

The Inspector, therefore, symbolises the position of socialists during the early 20th century who believed it necessary that society as a whole took a critical stance towards the attitudes and behaviours of the ruling classes. When the Inspector suggests

47

that those in power – those that assume the right to enjoy an untarnished reputation despite their conduct – are at fault, he calls into question the status quo that has masked the misdemeanours of the rich and powerful for centuries. As stated above, the examples given present the Inspector making these criticisms without being overtly direct, and speaking generally about society. Although this allows the Inspector to begin his investigation without an overly confrontational tone, it also enables Priestley to communicate to the audience his political agenda, encouraging the audience to think beyond the lives of the characters on the stage; the character of the Inspector is a vehicle for Priestley to awaken or nurture the audience's socialist convictions.

Another reason for why the Inspector is important to the play is because his character is instrumental in raising the narrative's tension. This rising tension is created through the Inspector becoming increasingly threatening as the drama unfolds. As stated above, initially, the Inspector's criticisms of Gerald and the Birlings are couched in broad accusations which appear concerned with society rather than the characters specifically. However, in later acts, the Inspector becomes more confrontational with individual characters. For example, in act two, he scolds Mrs Birling by telling her 'I think you did something terribly wrong' when she claims to be blameless. Soon after, the stage directions describe how the Inspector 'turns on' Mr Birling – the writer's choice of verb implying a sense of hostility – at which point the Inspector admonishes Mr Birling with the following lines: 'Don't stammer and yammer at me again, man. I'm losing all patience with you people.' Here, the language infers the Inspector's aggravation and anger towards Mr Birling: the imperative 'don't stammer' shows the Inspector asserting his authority over Mr Birling; the belittling mode of address – 'man' – reveals his lack of respect for Mr Birling; and the plosive alliteration in 'patience' and 'people' enhances the sense of irritation in the Inspector's voice.

The tension continues to rise until the Inspector exits in act three, threatening the characters with a lesson that 'will be taught... in fire and blood and anguish'. This polysyndeton repeats the connective 'and' to emphasise the extent of the punishment that will befall those who fail to conform to a socialist ideology. Here, the tension climaxes to its peak as the Inspector uses his final lines to deliver a threat that infers eternal damnation through the image of 'fire', as well as pain, suffering and death through the images of 'blood and anguish'.

The ratcheting up of tension through the Inspector's increasingly belligerent language, reflects the anger socialists felt for those in the ruling classes whose resistance to change was symptomatic of their apathy towards their victims and their selfish desire to maintain an undeserved sense of social superiority. Perhaps the character of the Inspector betrays Priestley's anger and frustration with such people, whose resistance stifled or blocked the progression of the socialist movement. Being set in 1912 but written in 1945, the final threatening lines of the Inspector undoubtedly allude to the terror of both world wars, thus inferring that a world which is able to embrace the central tenets of socialism is a world that is less inclined to find itself entangled in global warfare. Modern audiences may, on reflection, view Priestley's suggestion that a global socialist movement could have prevented two world wars as unconvincing and lacking perspicacity. Alternatively, if the reference to 'fire and blood and anguish' is solely alluding to a form of hell, it could be inferred that Priestley considered socialism to be a political stance that is harmonious with the Christian faith, with capitalism, therefore, being inherently profane.

Finally, the Inspector's sympathies for the disadvantaged members of society is integral to the play because it models the values and attitudes that Priestley desires to strengthen in his audiences. The Inspector's pity for Eva Smith, and those like her, is communicated early on in act 1 when he invites the others to try 'to put [themselves] in the place of these young women counting their pennies in their dingy little back bedrooms'. The Inspector's language is intentionally emotive here, with, for example, the adjective 'young' conveying a sense of vulnerability, and the adjective 'dingy' communicating the drab depravity in which such women were trapped. It is important to note that the writer is extending the Inspector's sympathies beyond the character of Eva Smith, projecting him as a man of socialist principles. Later, in the Inspector's final speech, these socialist principles are voiced clearly when he didactically states that 'one Eva Smith has gone – but there are millions and millions and millions of Eva Smiths and John Smiths still left with us, with their lives, their hopes and fears, their suffering and chance of happiness...'. Here, the Inspector appears to recalibrate the purpose of his visit for the other characters: it is not merely to expose the depravity of the wrongs they have committed in their interactions with Eva Smith, and therefore exact some form of social justice for Eva Smith; it is to re-educate those characters through learning by their mistakes in that they may develop a social conscience that has a tangible effect on the future.

While the Inspector fails in his mandate with Gerald, Mr Birling and Mrs Birling, Priestley seeks success in awakening his audiences' sympathies for the disadvantaged members of society. Through having the Inspector extend his sympathies beyond the character of Eva Smith, Priestley intends to remind audiences, persistently throughout the play, that social inequality was a wide-scale issue. This enhances the symbolic nature of the characters – for example, Eva Smith being representative of the enslaved working class and Mr Birling being symbolic of the covetous capitalist system. And by amplifying the symbolism at work in the play, through the character of the Inspector, Priestley intends to send a powerful message to his audiences regarding the plight of the disadvantaged and how they should be react to it. In order, therefore, to fully understand and appreciate the play, we must recognise the writer's intention is to politicise his audience as much as it is to entertain his audience.

[7] <u>Eva Smith</u>

Explore the importance of Eva Smith in *An Inspector Calls*.

You must refer to the context of the play in your answer.

Eva Smith is important to the play because she is a positive portrayal of a lower class woman. Crucial to this positive portrayal is her moral integrity and bravery which is conveyed during different characters' interrogations. For example, during Mr Birling's interrogation he describes Eva Smith as one of the 'ring-leaders, who'd started the trouble' and as having 'had a lot to say – far too much'. Although Mr Birling's intention is to render Eva a troublemaker, audiences who understood that, in 1912, the working class laboured in appalling conditions and earned barely enough to survive would have warmed to her character: such an audience would consider her a leader – someone who was unafraid to speak out for others and challenge the economic injustices suffered by her and her colleagues.

However, arguably, it is during Eric's interrogation that Eva Smith's moral fortitude is best highlighted. When Eva realised that the money with which Eric provided her was stolen, 'she wouldn't take any more, and she didn't want to see [him] again'. It is important to remember that in refusing to accept Eric's financial support, and by disassociating herself with him because of his criminality, Eva Smith chose a life of deprivation that put her life, as well as her unborn child's life, at risk; her choice was one that was guided by her moral principles, regardless of the dangers the decision imposed upon herself. Clearly, through Eva Smith's bravery and moral fortitude, Priestley intends to create a contrast between her and the characters that exploited her weaknesses.

Of course, Eva Smith is presented as victim, but through such moments as those discussed above, Priestley is able to establish her as a strong and stoic character – heroic even. With Eva Smith's symbolic status, representing the working class and lower class women, it was important for Priestley to avoid portraying her as simply a character to be pitied; the writer's socialist principles meant he favoured a portrayal that emphasised the value and strengths of people within these demographics – for Priestley, these were citizens whose worth had been overlooked and undervalued by politicians and the upper classes throughout history. Indeed, it can be stated that while Priestley is keen to expose the arrogant apathy of the ruling class, he is similarly keen to venerate the lower class.

Interestingly, although the Birlings and Gerald each mistreated Eva Smith, most of these characters are still shown to find her attractive. The most obvious example is Gerald who conveys his physical attraction to her when describing how 'she was very pretty – soft brown hair and big dark eyes'. Eric similarly describes her as 'pretty', and Mr Birling also comments on her attractive appearance: 'She was a lively good-looking girl – country-bred, I fancy'. Here, although Mr Birling praises her appearance, the adjective 'country-bred' implies a sense of contempt for her background, conjuring images of livestock. Sheila also considered Eva Smith 'a very pretty girl' which, she admits, catalysed her jealousy and led her to misuse the power of her upper-class status to force Eva's dismissal. It is important to recognise that Eva Smith's beauty is not merely a trivial aspect of her characterisation – in regards to her interactions with Sheila, Gerald and Eric, it could be considered Eva's fatal flaw. Had Eva Smith not been someone that the male characters physically desired, and had she not been someone whose beauty aggravated Sheila's low self-esteem, she would not have been exploited by them. By making Eva Smith's beauty her fatal flaw, Priestley exonerates her from holding any responsibility for the way she is mistreated by these three characters; it is their lust or

Laurie Ashwell

spite for her beauty that perpetuates her suffering.

Eva Smith's character is highly symbolic - she represents the struggles of the lower class and the victimisation that her class, and those of her gender, regularly suffered at the hands of the ruling class. By making Eva Smith's fatal flaw her beauty, Priestley is not only, once again, presenting a positive portrayal of the lower class, but emphasising their innocence in their suffering. Symbolically, Gerald and Eric's lust for her beauty implies a sinister dynamic that existed between middle and upper class men, with women of the lower class in 1912 – these were the women upon whom they preyed, intending that their sexual indiscretions remained concealed by the class division. Because the class division created a social division, it was rare that acts of adultery or abuse, committed by the middle and upper class men, were exposed.

Furthermore, in regards to Sheila's jealous reaction to Eva Smith's beauty, perhaps Priestley was intending to communicate the notion that the middle and upper classes are prone to impulsive and ill-considered reactions when their arrogant belief in their own superiority is undermined. Eva Smith's beauty undermined Sheila's belief in her own superiority, and perhaps Priestley intends her reactions to be considered indicative of the petulant and arrogant behaviour of her class.

Finally, and perhaps most obviously, Eva Smith is important to the play because she is presented as a victim of the ruling class – a victim of the inequality that pervaded society in the early twentieth century. However, it is crucial to remember that Eva Smith is a victim of a different kind of social injustice with each character that wrongs her. For example, Mr Birling's treatment of Eva Smith and his other employees as 'cheap labour' renders her a victim of capitalism, needing to survive on insufficient wages with poor job security. Here, Priestley intends to highlight the plight of the working class caused by the exploitation of the profit-driven capitalists who control British industry.

Eva Smith becomes Sheila's victim when Sheila coerces the manager of Milwards to 'get rid of' Eva Smith. However, here Eva Smith is not a victim of capitalism, but the petulance of the ruling class. This time, Priestley is showing the ruling class' inclination to misuse the power that accompanies its social status, and its inclination to persecute the lower class without good reason, regret or a thought for the consequences.

It could be argued that Mrs Birling similarly victimises Eva Smith, especially when considering her reaction to Eva Smith 'impertinently [making] use of [her] name'. But, there are other elements at play when Mrs Birling obstructs Eva from receiving assistance from her charity: her preconceived opinions of 'a girl of that sort' whom, as Mrs Birling believes, couldn't have 'elaborate fine feelings and scruples' infers a prejudicial treatment of the lower class – a belief in lower class people's inherent inferiority. This leaves those in desperate circumstances victims of the ruling class' apathy. Furthermore, if we consider the symbolic nature of an organisation failing in its duty to offer support where support was needed, it could be argued that Priestley is also shining a light upon the failings of conservative governments who, as socialists believed, persistently failed in their responsibility to address the plight of the lower class; symbolically, at least, Eva Smith is a victim of politicians' apathy.

As previously stated, Eva Smith is a victim of Gerald and Eric's lust. With Eric, this lust leads to rape, leaving Eva Smith a victim of sexual violence. Here, an abusive and clandestine facet of men's behaviour towards women is signified by Priestley – Eric's victimisation of Eva is, symbolically, a stark criticism of the commonality of sexual abuse directed at disadvantaged women by over privileged men in British society in the early twentieth century; this abuse is a perverse criminal symptom of the division between the different classes combined with the inequality between the genders.

Although lust similarly initiated the relationship between Gerald and Eva Smith, the dynamic in this relationship was different: as the Inspector notes, '[Gerald] at least had some affection for her and made her happy for a time'. Yet, perhaps, we could view the relationship through the lens of political symbolism again. Gerald provided economic support and comfort for Eva Smith while they were together, but when he decided to end the relationship, it was not long before Eva Smith once again found herself in poverty, frequenting the Palace Bar – 'a favourite haunt of women of the town'. Eva Smith's sudden and inevitable decline following the loss of the financial support that Gerald had provided could be considered symbolic of Priestley's fears for the future – if labour were to win the 1945 election and establish the welfare state, as indeed they did, would this support, and could this support, be ripped out from beneath the feet of the lower class, by politicians in the future? The loss of support experienced by Eva Smith and her plunge back into destitution could, therefore, symbolise Priestley's fears for the lower class becoming a victim of a political reversal against socialism in the future.

Laurie Ashwell

Printed in Great Britain
by Amazon